MW01488380

ANGEL MESSAGES

Breathe and Lift in Angelic Love,

Light & Compassion

ANGEL MESSAGES

Breathe and Lift in Angelic Love,
Light & Compassion

MELANIE BECKLER

www.Ask-Angels.com

"Regardless of your age, personal history, gender, religion or beliefs, you have angels who are willing to work with you at all times. Right now powerful help from the inner realms has been made available to you. Guides and angels stand by to work with you to bring healing into your life. You are able to make a difference in each moment. Choose love, choose hope and begin to plant the seeds of intention about what you desire to see manifest in your new beginning, in the new Earth. Set positive intentions, ask for help, and take action as you are inspired. Be willing to let go of the old to let new blessings in, for now is the time to rebirth yourself into experiencing the full divine love that you are. You are love…and you are so loved."

~Archangel Michael as channeled by Melanie

CONTENTS

Invocation to Connect

Here is a simple process to begin tuning into your inner soul voice and the love and frequency broadcast from the angels throughout the pages of this book.

I now invite you to join me in taking a deep relaxing breath, as you begin to focus your awareness within. Breathe, relax, and allow your heart to open.

Now feel or imagine that your energy is flowing down and grounding into the core of the Earth. You can imagine roots flowing down from the bottom of your feet, or just feel your conscious awareness drop in and flow down, where you are now able to connect with the light of the core of the Earth. Feel this connection with the Earth and with divine light. Feel that you are one with the light and one with all.

Now let this light from the core of the Earth flow up. Let it enter in through the bottom of your feet. Let it open all your chakra energy centers and continue to lift now in awareness with this light. Up and out of the crown chakra at the top of your head, above your higher energy centers above the lights, go up, seek and lift into a place of direct presence with source, with God, with the Divine. Feel the divine light present and flowing throughout this place now, connected to you and to all. Breathe and allow yourself to feel your oneness with the light of the Divine.

Now think or say:

> I now invite my highest, best, most loving possible guides, angels and ascended masters, please come in. Lift my vibration and assist me in opening my heart and entering in, so I may feel, hear, see, sense and know the presence of divine love in this moment and in every moment. Help me to clearly see my path and to know that I am guided and protected. Help me to live my authentic truth and accomplish the highest possible purpose for my life. Thank you.

Open your heart, consciously enter in, and then lift in the unconditional love that is broadcast now from the inner realms.

I now invite the highest, best, most loving possible guides, angels or ascended masters with truth, wisdom and knowledge to share, for the highest and greatest good of all; please come in, connect, and channel through me now.

1

Letting Go and Connecting
with Your Soul Light

~Archangel Haniel

*"Focus your intention now, from amidst this heart-centered place.
Know that we, in the divine realms, hear your plea and will
answer."*

~ *Archangel Haniel*

Dearest one, indeed I, Archangel Haniel, greet you in this very moment. Know that you are surrounded in a circle of light, with ascended masters, angels, Reiki ascended masters, healing guides, your team of guardian angels and guides who have been with you from the time of your birth, and some new guides who have joined you along your path as you found new interests and inspirations.

We are all here with you now, for one purpose, one express reason, and that is to assist you in releasing whatever attachments you have. Whatever you are holding on to, we are here to assist you in letting go. Surrender to the flow, to the process of life, so your full light and new waves of inspiration, healing, compassion, and joy may enter into your being. The process is simple. Let your mind be still and calm. And now let your heart be awakened and opened. Let the doors of your heart open and enter in. Drop in, sync in, breathe inwards.

The realm of spirit of your angels, guides and your team enters in. We are always a breath away. When you quiet your mind, when you center, and when you open your heart, you are able to enter in. Good. Now lift, relax and let more light that we broadcast flow into your being.

Let light seek out and bring up negativity and density, which is still stagnant and still held within your being. Let this rise to the surface so that we angels are able to wrap you in light and release these negative thoughts or vibrations, or perhaps even intentions, into the Creator's light. This energy that is connected to everything and all that is, when released, may be cleansed and purified and may return to the physical plane in a manner that will serve all.

This is our intention, the intention of the beings of light and ascended masters and angels who serve on the inner planes. We are committed to assisting you in lifting, in moving beyond the duality, struggle and density of the physical realm.

As you continue living, you may still be experiencing some struggle and challenge in your life. If this happens, when dense emotions come up, do not judge them. Release attachment. Release the need to react. Let it be OK. If sadness comes up, let it out. Let tears flow from your eyes and know that this very act is a release. But do not hold on to the pain, for that will simply allow it to latch on again; release.

Let the emotion go and think, Angels, take this from me. And we gladly will. We lift out of your aura, out of your physical body, and out of your light body anything that does not serve you on the path of becoming the full spiritual being and light that you are. This is of paramount importance and it is an essential reason why you are here: to clear out past density you have experienced so far in your Life, or density you have experienced in your past lives, where tragedy or struggle were truly felt by you as a soul. But at this powerful point of being in between time, the past is able to wash away. If you are willing, you are able to release it and lift to a new level.

For when density, harsh emotions and negativity no longer weigh you down, you are able to lift in the light. And through lifting, combined with your soul light lowering down, you are able to merge with your full spirit in the physical. This is all made possible by the simple act of quieting your mind, opening your heart and entering in. There, within your open heart, you are able to access infinite realms.

We encourage you, from this portal of your heart, to lift and to connect with divine love. For divine love not only serves you in bringing more joy and love and compassion to others, but in your experience and in your life, love will align you with healing, with vibrant health and well-being and with the ability to live life, thriving in joy, love and abundance.

You see, as a soul, you knew there would be struggle in this Earth on which you were born. You knew you were entering into a realm of duality and density. But, through your action and intention, you can now turn away from the old ways of responding and relating. Those negative patterns and habits you picked up from family or friends or the media. Now is the time to let those things go. You may ask, how do you do this?

Again, the process is simple. Quiet your mind. Feel your energy ground and feel your connection to the Earth and to all that is. Then open your heart and enter in. From this space, all the love of the Divine is available to you. How would you like to integrate divine love into your life?

Do you desire healing? Or do you desire abundance? Focus your intention now, from amidst this heart-centered place. Know that we, in the divine realms, hear your plea and will answer. Simply being in this love and light will bring you many benefits. A huge shift will come when you truly let go of the past, when you find completion, when you reflect on your life thus far, accepting what has been. This doesn't mean you have to be OK with what has been, but just accept it.

From this acceptance, you can move forward in love and in joy for the highest and greatest good. You can bring light into your life to benefit your experience, but it ends not there. For in every moment, remember you are connected to everyone. So as you evolve, as you ascend, as you begin to respond to challenges and blessings and struggles in the same way, with love and with compassion, you enter into the new paradigm. You become a leader and a way-shower: one who is leading the masses in integrating the new paradigm into Earth.

What is this new paradigm you speak of, Archangel Haniel? Beloved one, I say to you now that it is the paradigm of love, the reign of love, a life filled with love. Love—feel this radiate throughout your being. Love has the power to inspire, the power to heal, and the power to evolve.

This is where you are now: healing, evolving and lifting in love to reunite with the full authentic being you are, a physical being at this time. Yes, a physical being who is fully aware and united with the full spiritual light, the full authentic self, aware of the higher self and soul that you are.

Imagine now that an incredible light hovers above you. This is the light of your soul and it begins to lower down. Consciously think yes to allow this. Open your crown, your mind, your heart, and feel your energy bump up in frequency. Feel your vibration increase from making this link with your soul.

Now, filled with light in a manner that you can then overflow to the world around you and to others, once more feel your energy ground. Witness light flowing down through the bottom of your feet, so the incredible light of the Divine, which you have absorbed and integrated, is now grounded into the planet, into Earth and all that is.

This process serves you and all whom you are energetically and physically connected to. So make it a daily priority moving forward to clear your mind, to open your heart, and to let your soul light merge with you in the physical, grounding your light in to Earth. This benefits you and all that is.

Know that the blessings you bring into the lives of others, the service you provide here in the physical, return to you multiplied. The service, the love, the lessons will stay with your soul and with your spirit forever. So, make the most of this time. The time is now. Let go and release that which is outdated and no longer serves you. Enter in and lift to embrace a new level of becoming, a new level of light. Experience a new level of truth about who you are, dear physical being, a powerful spiritual light.

I, Archangel Haniel, now invite you once more to feel your energy ground to the Earth. All of this light from the Divine, from the ascended masters, and from your guides and your angels can be integrated into your life by simply feeling with your conscious awareness, feeling your energy flow down, so that all this light merges with the Earth and with all that is.

This is powerful work you are doing, and it serves you and all. So prioritize and daily take time to quiet your mind, ground your energy, open your heart and connect. For we will always answer; we are so pleased to be of assistance. And you are so loved. Share this love. Overflow with love. For love will lead and guide you always.

We are always near. Call upon angelic assistance and we will answer. I, Archangel Haniel, now leave you with another infusion of love and light. Let it in and ground it to receive full benefit of this light of the Divine in your physical life and reality. And so, it is. And so, it shall be.

I now leave you with my blessing. Goodbye for now.

2

Through Love
All Things Are Possible

~Archangel Metatron

"Love heals a wounded heart. Love heals a damaged body. Love heals a scattered mind."

~ Archangel Metatron

Beloved, indeed I, Archangel Metatron, am here. You are greeted in this very moment with a wave of frequency broadcast from the Divine. Indeed, this wave of light energy, particles of high vibrational atoms of the light, flows your way in order to lift you out of any perceived barriers. To lift you out of the realm of doubt, of uncertainty, and into knowing, understanding, and being fully aware that you are love, light, and well-being.

Through these forces of divine intelligence, you are connected to all—including, your higher self and spirit still present in the realms above, and including your guides and angels, who are always near, watching over you, protecting and assisting you.

One vibrational force energy is flowing throughout creation that you are a part of. What this means is that with your intention and awareness, you are able to focus and formulate this frequency in order to create in your world. Indeed, this is of paramount importance. It is why you are here in the physical at this time: in order to create blessings.

But let us rewind for a moment and look at things from a slightly different perspective of how you entered into this realm. You see, before you were born, you were complete in spirit, completely connected to the realms of divine love and source. Aware of your oneness with this love vibration, and because you were complete in love, well-being and hope, you chose to see an opportunity upon planet Earth—a planet plagued by fear and doubt and control. And you, dear light being, brave warrior of love, chose to enter into density, to forget your true light, and ultimately your full power, so you could enter into the physical realm, knowing you would remember. With this remembrance, you would have the ability to create lasting change, to tip the scales away from fear and control towards the new paradigm, the new experience on planet Earth, which is living centered in compassion and love.

Now that you are here in the physical, the challenges associated with this mission may seem overwhelming at times. But we say to you, you are never alone. You are always supported. There is truly an unlimited amount of support available to you, beyond the veil, beyond the realm of the physical, entering into energy, into spirit. You see, as you connect with your own spirit, your own inner light, all the power of the spiritual realms becomes available to you. And you are able to focus this in a way, in a manner, and in a mode to change your circumstance, to change your luck.

There is much talk in your realm about the Law of Attraction, about your thoughts creating your reality. The essence of this is true; however, it is much more complicated than to simply think it, and so, it is. For laws are influenced by many different factors. By thinking positively about something you want, while your subconscious, outside of your awareness, is worried about what you do not want, you can see, in this scenario, your energy being pulled in two directions. And so in this way, we angels bring you subconscious healing.

At this time, you may relax and know that you are safe and dearly loved. We are simply here to assist you in taking the next step forward into vibrant living, a step towards thriving here on Earth in physical form.

As I, Archangel Metatron, speak these words, many other guides and ascended masters and beings of great light on the inner planes enter into this space and time. For your focused awareness, your open heart creates a vortex of sorts, a powerful energetic opening by which we are able to flow frequency of blessing in to your experience.

Allow yourself to simply be present, as now we angels lower down an orb of high vibrational blue-and-green healing light from above. Imagine that this healing orb lowers down all around your physical body, first, bringing healing energy, to your physical form. Feel yourself open up to allow this healing energy in and let it flow wherever you are most in need. Wherever there is pain or blocked energy or discontent, this energy flows its way now to release stuck energy, to release pain into the light. And now, like a shock wave flowing in and shaking things up, any remaining fear, anxiety, density or doubt still stored in your physical body, in your cellular memory is released.

Archangel Michael swoops in now with a giant vacuum that is placed over your crown chakra. Feel the updraft of energy as fear, uncertainty, doubt, anxiety, and worry are vacuumed away, vacuumed out, sucked out from the core of each and every one of your trillions of cells, which make up your physical body. Wherever fear has been stored, fear has now been released. Let it go willingly, openly. You may feel your energy tighten a bit, or twitch, or tense. Whatever you are feeling, let this be a validation that this cleanse is indeed happening. Divine light is releasing that which no longer serves the truth of who you are authentically in spirit.

You are one with that which is light and love. You are a powerful being, able to manifest blessings of healing, abundance, hope and joy in your reality by letting go of the worry and fear you have absorbed thus far in your life, through experiences, challenges, and lessons. Now let it go.

We angels now release from a new orb of golden light above you, a waterfall, which begins to flow down. A waterfall of light washing away any residue with the gentle elements of wind and rain, clearing out all that no longer serves. Good. Now, open your heart and, with a new level of lightness at your core, allow yourself to lift. Allow yourself, through your conscious awareness, to lift up and out of your physical body. Up and out of the dense and sometimes challenging realm of the physical, so that right now you are floating. You are lifting up and into a sacred space.

Know that you are able to reach this space by focusing within your heart and then lifting in consciousness. And so, open your heart and feel the immense amount of love available for you right now. Love from the Divine, love of the highest order, love that has the ability to turn your life around, to refocus your mind, your body, your spirit on your ultimate path and divine blueprint. This is the essence of why you are here: why you as a powerful spiritual being chose to enter into the present physical reality. You are here to impart lasting change upon this planet.

Through love, all things are possible, and all manner of creating blessings in your world are opened. It is remarkable that there are so few words to express the full meaning of love. Love has the power to heal and the power to create. As you allow more love into your body, into your cellular memory, now your body absorbs this love in the mode of healing. Love heals a wounded heart. Love heals a damaged body. Love heals a scattered mind. Love, the most powerful force available to you here in the physical, holds the key to creating the blessings you seek.

And yet, there is a challenge for you in staying in love, despite whatever is happening around you in the physical world. When you are challenged or judged or criticized by others, being able to stay in a position of loving yourself is not easy. The love you feel for yourself, the love from your inner-realm is mirrored through the outer world around you. If you are attracting challenges in your life, you may think, How have I created this? This is not what I really desire. Return to love for it is the absence of love for yourself that causes your outer reality to mirror this absence of love.

There is a belief stored in the collective consciousness of humanity that God is to be feared and loved. However, God will only love you when you are good, and when you are bad, that love is taken away. You see, this belief is centered in control, in trying to get you to fear, to question making changes for fear of upsetting the creator of all, God, goddess, light.

At this time, with your willingness, we are able to release this limiting belief. Watch it go. Let it go. Witness it being released into the light, and now being replaced with the belief, with the feeling, with the knowing that I am unconditionally loved regardless of my actions. I am unconditionally loved regardless of the outcome. I am unconditionally loved, and I live in a loving and supportive multiverse.

From our perspective, this is completely true. You see, we have an unlimited amount of love for you, dear beloved spiritual being in physical form. Tune into even a small fraction of this, and let yourself feel the same way. Let yourself recognize that the core of who you are, the spirit of who you are is complete love and is always connected to the Divine, to the oneness flowing throughout all that is, to all that is. Love is your essence.

When you experience things that point you away from love, such as fear, you can choose to let it go like dropping a pencil. You have free choice to walk away from a challenging situation. You are responsible for your energy in every moment. It is your energy in every moment that creates your outside experience. Your inner world is mirrored by the outer world around you.

You are able to heal your inner world and remain centered in love, in hope, in the light. When you are able to believe that the universe is conspiring with you to accomplish your goals, and that love is present in everyone and everything; when you love, you step onto the accelerated path of bringing about blessings.

How you believe and how you feel about situations largely

dictate the results about how they will unfold. This is why you may have a friend who seems naturally lucky, for they believe they are lucky. Their inner realm, their inner state of being believes they are lucky, and the outer world simply mirrors this natural belief.

Beliefs are interesting because they are ingrained in you from the time of your birth, from your parents, from your teachers, from your society. Yet you have the ability to change your beliefs, and the process is essentially simple. It involves first connecting with the oneness flowing throughout all that is. You are able to do this by quieting your mind. For it is with your heart, and not your mind, that you are able to unlock the secrets of the universe, of the Divine.

And so now, quiet your mind and open your heart; center your awareness and enter in. Ground and feel yourself present in physical reality. Feel roots extending down from the bottom of your feet, anchoring you in to the Earth. As this happens, notice that you are not separate from Earth. The atoms and the molecules that make up you also make up Earth. You are connected.

Feel this connection, feel this light, and then let it flow up and let it open all of your chakras; the light healing and balancing your earth chakra, root, sacral, solar plexus, your heart, your throat, your crown, your soul star chakra above the top of your head. And continuing to lift up, like a door to the Divine has been opened, and indeed it has. It is your birthright to make this connection directly with source for yourself, to lift on wings of love and connect directly with source and with the Divine.

Lift now, through your open heart, through your open crown, through your open mind. Lift into the light. Good. Feel the immense love for you, which is present here now, and accept this love. Let it in for you are one with it. You are a part of love, you are all. You are in direct presence with divine source, prime source, creative source, goddess, God, light, and the Divine. Open your heart and enter in to the still, silent, calm connection in this way.

Then you may ask, what belief is present in me that does not serve my ultimate truth? Listen, be aware. Notice what comes into your mind. Notice what you hear, how you feel. Be aware. What beliefs are you operating with that no longer serve you? Let this rise to the surface and let it go. Your guardian angel takes it, lifts it out of your being, and releases it into the Light. Witness this. And now, let this belief be replaced with an empowering belief, with something that does serve you in aligning with your truth, with your highest possible purpose. Let this empowering belief take its place.

We now ask on your behalf, "What do you need to release from your life, from your thoughts and from your beliefs in order to accomplish your highest possible purpose? "Know that your angels are here to assist you in to tuning into this knowledge. What do you need to release? Is it fear? Is it negative thinking? Is it something more specific? Be aware.

Imagine you are writing down on a piece of paper the things that you are ready to release from your life. Now a glowing orb of fire appears before you—a violet fire, the violet flame of transmutation. Put your paper of what you are ready to release into this flame as a way of handing it over to the Divine to handle the details. As your paper ignites and releases, so too are these things able to release from your life. Now the violet orb of high vibrational frequency, of divine fire moves around you, gently burning away all that no longer serves you in accomplishing your highest possible purpose. Self-doubt, fear, anger, and anxiety …let these go. With a whoosh, the angels take them into the light of the Divine.

And now, where these were contained, begin filling the void with love, the most powerful force available to you in the multiverse; love enters in to fill the gap. Your aura, your energetic protection is now healed and restored with love, joy and compassion. As this protective shield becomes more intact, your vibration lifts. You are able to be less affected by the struggles experienced by others in the outside world around you. You are able to encounter challenges on your path and stay centered in love, hope and compassion.

These forces of the Divine surround you now. Know you have the express ability to invite them back in at any time by simply thinking, saying, being aware of love, hope and compassion. With awareness, these lights, these vibrational frequencies flow around you, protecting you but also healing your vibration, healing the energetic signature that you broadcast out in every moment, which intermingles with all that is and begins the process of creation in your world.

It is with love and compassion, with gratitude, that you attune your energy signature to bring you into alignment with what you love and appreciate. In this way when you give praise, when you rejoice in the successes of others, when you are able to appreciate blessings in others' lives, giving thanks and expressing how wonderful those things are, you open the door for such blessings to enter into your life as well.

Give thanks for all you have in your life, and this gratitude will magnify and bring more to be grateful for unto you.

Indeed, your inner state of being is mirrored in your outer reality. So challenging relationships with others simply shows you that there is still tension in your inner world and mind. Repeat the process of grounding, of connecting to the one life-force energy flowing throughout all that is. Bring light up through you to open all your chakras. Enter into the light and into direct presence with source. Once you are here, ask: What is holding me back? What do I need to let go of?

Quiet your mind and open your heart to know, to hear, to see, to sense, to smell and to experience the answer. Whatever subtle sense is most strengthened for you now, is how this answer will appear. If an idea simply pops into your head, accept this. Then you may think or say, Archangel Metatron, Archangel Michael, Angels, release this into the light and, in its place, flow love, compassion, well-being and hope.

Notice once more now, there is an orb of light above your head, shimmering, and sparkling. This unadulterated, complete essence of love lowers down around you. As this orb lowers around you, let it lift you to a new level and degree. Light lifts you by dismissing the doubt and struggle, which has been your past story, and by refocusing on where you are right now. You are at a powerful point of new beginning, a point of unlimited possibility.

For with love, all things are possible. All institutions have the ability to change with love. All challenges have the ability to be overcome with love. All illness and disease is able to be dissolved with pure love, which is all around you now. The love that is in you, that is around you, breathe in the love and let it fill your being. Now when you exhale, imagine you are releasing dense energy from you. Release that which is not love, and all that no longer serves.

Once more now, breathe in the love. Feel it cycling throughout your body, bringing healing to every cell, every muscle, every atom, so you are filled with love. You are overflowing with light and love, so now when you breathe out, love and light release. Breathe in love and light. Breathe out love and light. As you breathe in, let love cycle throughout your body, bringing healing to every inch. And as you breathe out, let your love flow outward into the world, bringing blessings to planet Earth and to all that is.

Know that your outer world is a mirror of your inner state of being, and the more you are able to love yourself and love others, the more love will return to you multiplied for healing, for abundance, for enlightenment. Ah yes, the highest possible reason for why you are here. Of course, your mission will take many specific turns and has layers of focus. However, the essence is to let your full spirit reunite here in the physical with your physical form. You are a master. You are a spiritual being.

Let this truth become known to you. Let yourself radiate love, compassion, hope and well-being from within; so it is without. As you love in the inner capacity, your outer world will shift around you. We angels are here to assist you in the entire process and encourage you to be not overwhelmed. Take one step, one breath, one moment at a time. As you return to love in your thoughts, words, and actions, everything shifts around to mirror back that which is within you.

So let your love shine bright and be bold. Take steps towards fulfilling the specifics of your mission by acting upon the subtle guidance and inspiration you receive. Taking even small steps now will multiply and lead to large, significant lasting changes, which will benefit this entire realm.

You are an earth angel, a spiritual being present in physical form. And as this becomes more and more known to you, the magnitude of what you are able to accomplish and change and heal so too increases as well. Your opportunity is now, and you are the one. Shine, love, and through this, the rest will be made known to you. Heal within and experience the blessings of this inner healing outside of you.

I, Archangel Metatron, am always near. Call upon me at any time for assistance. Know that you are so loved, and this love has the ability to heal and transform even the most corrupt and blatant challenges and atrocities in the physical realm. Love yourself fully and completely, and release anything that stands in your way of doing just that into the light. Love heals. Love is. And you are love. You are so loved.

We leave you with our blessing and with a final wave of frequency and light to illuminate you to a new level. Lift in this. Now feel your energy ground, anchoring this light and love and well-being into the Earth and into your physical life, for the highest and greatest good. And so, it is, and so, it shall be. I am complete for now. I leave you with unlimited blessings. Open your heart to receive.

3

Connect With Your
Guides and Angels

~Angel Guide Orion

"You have a life guide, your spirit guide who is with you for your entire life, and indeed, you have additional guides and angels who come in to help you here in the physical."

~ Orion

Beloved one, indeed, I am here. Some may call me an angel guide or spirit guide. I am Orion, and I am so pleased to connect with you in this very moment, for now is a time in which the realms of spirit and the realms of many multiple dimensions are available from planet Earth and are easily accessible. Now is a powerful new beginning in which you are able to consciously choose to recommit to your spiritual growth and the path of the open heart, the path of living love, the path of anchoring your spiritual light into physical form.

I, Orion, am pleased to be here now to assist you in strengthening your connection with your own spirit guides and angels who are always near you. Indeed, you have a guardian angel who has been with you from the time of your birth.

You have a life guide, your spirit guide, who is with you for your entire life. And indeed, you have additional guides and angels who come in to help you with particular challenges, missions, healing or for other purposes here in the physical.

Now it is my pleasure to first assist you in strengthening your connection with your guardian angel. To do this, relax, breathe, and let your mind quiet. Know that it is not in the realm of mind or thought that this connection will be made. There is guidance that can benefit your mind. You may even receive guidance from your guardian angel in the form of thought.

But to make and strengthen this connection, it is important to let the ego mind go. Imagine that you are setting your ego mind aside now, putting it on a shelf, and going inward and opening your heart. Let your mind focus on the words you read now, and let your heart become awakened, illuminated, and let it open.

Dear one, open your heart, and as you do, I, Orion, send light your way. Light of the highest form, high, fine light vibration to lift you up now, lifting you up in spirit and in consciousness to make the link, to make the connection with your guardian angel. We lift you up in vibration into the celestial angelic realm.

And so quiet your mind, open your heart, and tune into your subtle psychic senses beneath the surface. These senses enable you to feel, see, hear, sense, and know beyond the veil. Use your inner mind's eye to see, and your inner ears to hear. Open these senses, tune into your feelings. The lightness, the love, the magnificence that is all around, let this flow all around you, let it flow in you, cleansing you, lifting you.

Now imagine that you are completely glowing with light, and you are surrounded with light. Indeed, a circle of angels surrounds you, broadcasting love now. You see, love is the most powerful force available for you to make this link. And so, open your heart, quiet your mind, and then say or think repeating these words in your mind, I now invite my highest, best, most loving guardian angel to come in, connect with me now. And notice your guardian angel does come in now over your right shoulder, a loving presence, a light-filled presence of high, fine beautiful vibration. Open your heart, quiet your mind, tune into your subtle senses, and open the doors of your heart wide. Good. Your guardian angel is present with you now.

And we ask on your behalf, "What message do you have at this time?" Open to receive this blessing of guidance and of energy, for your guardian angel, who has been with you throughout your life, knows your challenges, your secrets, your struggles, as well as your accomplishments and your successes, and loves you all the same amidst your highest and lowest points. Quiet your mind, and listen with your heart to hear or feel the message.

Nothing but unconditional love is felt for you by your guardian angel. Know that you are safe in their presence. And we now ask, "Dear guardian angel, do you have a gift at this time to give to assist in the strengthening of a path of spiritual and personal growth?"

Open your heart to receive this gift from your guardian angel. Do you receive a mental image, a thought or a word? Do you receive an overwhelming feeling of being loved? Your guardian angel gives you whatever is most important for you to receive at this time. Let it in, accept it, and give your thanks. Your guardian angel will remain now over your right shoulder, always with you, and ready to assist. Call upon your guardian angel for assistance.

You may ask, dear guardian angel, what is your name? If you are ready to hear this, your angel may give you this information now; it will appear in your awareness. Do not worry if you do not receive a name. Just focus on opening your heart and making the connection. This is most important, for the full connection with your guardian angel will come in the time and pace that is right for you. You can accelerate your connection by choosing the path of an open heart. The more you love and ask to connect, the more you ask your guardian angel to help you make the connection, and the more you think of angels, imagine them, call upon them, the more this connection will strengthen.

And now, beloved one, I, Orion, once again broadcast a wave of frequency to lift you up. And above your left shoulder, we invite in the spirit guide or angel or star being who is on hand now to assist you in your purpose, in your current project, and with your current lessons that you are facing in this realm of physical reality. Let this guide come in.

Open your heart, quiet your mind, let your energy be big, and know that your guide too will assist you in making this link. You lift up in vibration, they lower down in vibration, and you meet in the middle. They connect with your heart chakra, your crown chakra, your third eye, and even your throat. And there is a place on the back of your head, a point where they may place their hand or energy to assist you in making the link. If you feel any sort of pressure, if your heart is pounding wildly, let this all be OK. Let it be a validation that, indeed, this guide is present with you now. Your energy is being lifted to make the connection with your guide.

We now ask on your behalf, "What can you share that will most serve at this time?" Clear your mind, open your heart, and receive this guidance, this love. And is there a gift that this guide has for you now? Open to receive and notice what it is they give to you now that will most help you in overcoming your current lessons and challenges. And now we ask, "Beloved one, will you share your name?"

Another surge of light and frequency now flows your way. Let it open all your chakra energy centers, reconnecting you with the divine sacred pattern for your chakra psychic and spiritual centers. Now uniting each chakra along your spine in one vibrant white light, a pillar of light, it allows you to be illuminated and fully aware.

Now we invite in your life guide, your spirit guide for life, who was with you before you were born and who will be with you here on Earth to assist you in your life mission and purpose until the time you die. Often this is someone you have known in a past life, or you have only known them in the realm of spirit, but they're always with you, connecting with you now from above the top of your head.

You have your guardian angel on your right shoulder, your current angel or guide on your left, and now your life guide comes in over the top of your head. And as you make the link, an incredible light pours in through your crown chakra.

Open your heart and make this connection with your life guide, who loves you dearly and who is always on hand to assist you in anything, but especially with knowing your purpose and your path in spirit.

And so, open your heart, your crown, your third eye, and let your ego mind set aside. Open and think or say, I now invite my highest, best, most loving possible life spirit guide, who was with me at the time of my birth and is still with me now, come in and connect.

Dearest one, open and feel this link, this connection that indeed is made now. Your guide is present, and so, we ask, "What guidance do you have for this beloved being now about how they may link more fully with spiritual growth, with their spiritual path, and full purpose?"

Open your heart and you may, at first, only feel this response, this overwhelming love and light and vibration; float and lift with it. Let it in. Let yourself open to it, for indeed, it is here to serve you and to illuminate you and to help reunite you with why you are really here, with your purpose as a spiritual being in physical form. This is multifaceted, yes, but tune into a current facet of this, your highest purpose, and what next is important for you to progress.

Your guide focuses their energy and speaks to you now through your psychic sense, which is currently most illuminated, whether that is in the form of a feeling, a mental image, sensing, hearing the guidance, or simply coming into your awareness. Whatever you receive, let it be OK. Open your heart, let love in.

We now ask your life spirit guide, "Do you have a gift, a tool for this beloved, whatever will most serve now?" What gift or tool does your guide give you now? Become aware, and if it feels good and right, accept this gift. Integrate it into your aura and your energy, and give thanks to your life guide who is present with you. Now we ask your guide to do whatever will most serve you in strengthening your connection. Let this in.

And finally, beloved life guide, "What is your name?" Drop into your heart, let it open, quiet your mind, and from the still calm voice within, the name of your guide may emerge. Or they may choose to give you an image of what they look like, or a vibrational signature you can think of to invite them in. Receive whatever your guide gives you.

Now draw your awareness to this divine trio with you now, these three guides who can most serve you in your current circumstance and path—your guardian angel, your spirit guide, and your life guide. We now invite these guides to flow your way whatever healing, whatever nurturing, and whatever love you most need.

Imagine now an orb of light forming around you, the color of whatever healing energy is most beneficial for you now. Notice the color, and then let this light from the Divine, from your guides, from the realms above flow through you. Let it take any pain or suffering or tragedy still held in your cellular memory. Let these be released into the light, and now open your heart and let love in.

Know, dearest one, that love is truly the master path that lies before you. As you are able to love in every moment, you are able to illuminate, you are walking your spiritual path, and the connection with your guides can ever be increased. You have work here to do together, though some may wish to call it play, for connecting with your spiritual guides feels good, is exciting and awakens your passions.

Open your heart, quiet your mind, and call in your guides. I now invite my highest, best, most loving possible, easiest guide to make this connection. Come in and connect with me now. Open your heart, feel your energy lift, and feel yourself connect. You can call upon your guides at any time, and we will answer. You can call upon me, Orion, at any time, and I will assist you in making the link with the Divine and with your guides who love you and can serve you on your path in life, and in accomplishing your purpose.

Dear one, you are here for greatness. You have felt this in the past at times and there is a reason. But do not be too hard on, or expect too much from, yourself, for greatness can simply be uniting with your full light of compassion and sharing this love, this kindness with all whom you meet. Love continues you forward on your path of spiritual growth and awakening. The more you love, the more your gifts come in, the more you open, and the more you lift, this serves. Connect with new levels of joy, love, and light in your life, and ground all this light, all this love, and these gifts you have received into physical form.

Now ground, feel your energy flowing down this tube of white light, uniting all your chakras. Let it flow down with your awareness below your feet and into the core of Mother Earth. Here at the core, feel the light, feel the love, and feel the well-being that Earth flows your way. Notice that Earth is connected with everything, with the one energy flowing throughout all that is, and so too are you. And so, feel this oneness and the healing and the light available therein at the core of the Earth.

Now that you are ready, now that you have sufficiently grounded the great light you received from your guides and from me, Orion, let your consciousness lift up once more, light flowing up, uniting all your chakras in a pillar of white light. Open your heart, and now allow yourself to return to the physical body and let whatever you experienced, be OK. Your guides did come in, your guides and angels did make the connection, which will continue to build and grow as you move forward.

But more than anything, remember, when you choose love, you are on your path of awakening. Love is the master path, the accelerated path of spiritual growth. Let love guide you and know that all is well. I, Orion, leave you with my blessing. Goodbye for now.

4

Express Your Creative Source Light

~Archangel Gabriel

"I am always near, and I am happy to assist you in cultivating your inner creativity, so you may use this to create blessings in your life and for the physical realm in general."

~ Archangel Gabriel

Dearest one, indeed I, Archangel Gabriel, greet you in this very moment. You are indeed in the presence of many beings of love and light. Know that we come simply to assist you in further lifting in the energy of love that is around, so you may rise out of the experience of struggle and density. And you may lift into fully expressing and being the true creative source light that you are, allowing this to fully shine here and now in this physical realm in which you reside.

And so, open your heart. As the love energy that is all around you cleanses you, let this love begin to pour in through the top of your head, letting it melt away tension, struggle and doubt. And let yourself lift so you may fully experience the truth that you are. You are a creative being of the light and you are here in the physical to create. This does not mean that everyone is meant to be a painter or an artist. Indeed creativity takes many forms. But you are here to create, first, in thought and intention, and then to bring these creations in to physical being, to physical reality through your actions.

Your intuitive nudges and inspirations serve, especially when you are in a place of meditation, when your heart is open and your mind is calm. Know that indeed the dreams, the intuitive nudges, and the direction you feel at a core level of where you ought to be heading, urge you toward your purpose. These intuitive nudges about how you can improve your life and the world around you are the very guidance your soul broadcasts in order to bring you into alignment with your path, with your divine blueprint, with the plan for your soul and spirit, which was laid out prior to your birth.

Know that, yes, there is a plan for your life. A divine plan, a divine blueprint; an idea about what you as a soul and spirit wanted to accomplish and experience, and even be challenged by here in the physical. For ultimately, you are here to learn and grow and evolve as a soul and a spirit. Although you have a plan and blueprint for your life, it is still up to you in the moment, in the now moment and in every moment to determine what you draw unto you.

For though there is a plan for your life, you still have free will. You have the option, the choice, in every moment. When something is going well for you, when you are in alignment in this way, you are feeling good, you are creating what you want, and the channel of abundance is open. Know that you will have the opportunity to turn the other way, to slip back into fear or doubt or insecurity.

You are encouraged to follow the nudging, the voice, and the guidance of your heart and of love. For love serves you well, and love will keep you in alignment with that which you desire to create, and who you desire to be. Love is the master path; for when you respond with love, there is healing through this as well. When you treat another with compassion, your vibration lifts so you are able to flow out even more compassion in the future. A ripple effect is started.

This is why we say to you, "Choose love in every moment." Not because we simply prefer watching you walk a road of satisfaction and fulfillment; yes, this is true. But ultimately, you are here to grow. You are here to learn, and you are here to integrate what you learn from the lessons of life into your being. This growth will stay with you forever, for your soul's journey onward, after this world, after this life and current experience.

The gifts, the spiritual light, and the tools you develop and practice, like meditation or your spiritual awakening, go with you. This does not end when you die but carries on indefinitely with you as a soul, as you travel and as you continue. Know that, yes, after this life of yours in the present, your soul will continue on—continue learning, lifting, and growing. And the actions you take in this life are setting the stage for your future incarnations and experiences.

And so, you ask why or how could one person be born into such poverty and hardship and tragedy, while another is born with everything? Why could one person be born into an abusive situation, while another who is loving and compassionate desires to have a child and cannot? How could this be? Again, it comes back to what you as a soul desired to experience in this life. There is some thought that your entire life is planned without you. But this is simply not the case.

Prior to your birth, you spent a great deal of time planning this current incarnation. It may upset some of you, but we say to you now that you chose this life you are in, and you chose the option to be presented with choices that would lead you towards many of the struggles and challenges and lessons you have learned thus far. If you wanted to only experience the high, fine and light vibrations, you would have stayed in the realm of spirit where you were prior to your birth.

But you, brave soul traveler, chose to enter into a realm known to have density still. For you knew that great learning for your soul would come about because of it. And you also knew that you would be able to remember the true source of your light. You would be able to see beyond the veil of illusion and remember that you are not separate from source, God, Heavenly Father, Mother Earth. You are indeed one— one vibration and energy with all.

Before you were born, you experienced this and knew this fully. And now that you are here, you can tune into that past wisdom and insight and ground your spiritual being, your light, your compassion and love, into the physical. For you are here to grow, to evolve and also to serve. Your service is perhaps the fastest way to evolve and grow. For when you serve and love, the benefits you receive are multiplied from that which you have sent out. And so, to serve and to love not only benefits those you are helping and loving. They do receive benefits, but you receive perhaps even more.

For love begins a wave, and the love you send out that touches another returns to you multiplied. When your act of kindness or compassion encourages them to help another, the love they send out causes another to feel love and compassion, and then pay it forward and help another. Thus the love of all of these interactions returns to each being and to you multiplied. Serving and loving others is your master path to awaken your light, to anchor your full spiritual self and voice here in the physical.

Again I will say, as you follow your intuitive nudges, as you follow your inner voice, as you respond with love and compassion, and as you practice quieting your mind and listening to your heart, you will be guided in which direction to go. You may be surprised at the guidance you receive, but when you begin to act on these nudges, act on this inspiration, and put aside your fear, you will bring about positive changes in your reality. You have this ability.

This is a large part of why you are here, creative creator—one with the Creator, one with all that is, and able to channel through you the light of the Divine, the light of your true and authentic spiritual self. When you do this, you pave the way towards alignment with who you really are, authentic soul spiritual being, here in present form to serve, to love, to lift yourself and to share this upliftment with others.

Right now, imagine there is an orb of light above your head. As all we guides and angels, who are here with you, flow our energy into this orb, light, cleansing love, and frequency from the Divine. Now this orb of light begins to lower down like a waterfall of light pouring down. When you simply open by relaxing, by focusing on your heart, this light pours all around you, dissolving away tension, anxiety and any cords of negativity, which connect you to others here in the physical and drain your energy. These cords are dissolved away into the light.

Any and all negativity you may have taken on by others is dissolved into the light. Light and love take its place, pouring into you, filling any gaps in your aura, lifting you in love, searching and flowing throughout your entire being. Any density that is encountered, any negativity or any entities are now released into this light for the highest and greatest good of you and of all. Let them go.

Let more light in and let yourself lift in this light, as it flows all throughout you, cleansing out the old to make way for the new cocreative journey before you. Your journey of creating in physical form, of taking your dreams, intentions and inspirations and asking your guides and angels and source for help. Then trusting, yes, you are receiving help, but not outside of your actions. And so take the actions as you are inspired, for you are always guided to make small improvements, to bring yourself into more health and vitality and abundance. Act upon the guidance you receive and know that you are capable of bringing about significant and lasting changes in this physical realm.

Currently, there is still density that has a stronghold on many people. But know that as you yourself walk this path of love, light and compassion, as you open fully to your light, and as you ground it into physical form all are affected. When density occurs outside you, when tragedy takes place in your world, we encourage you not to dwell on it, for this gives it energy. And where your attention goes, energy flows. And where your energy flows, that is strengthened. When you focus on what you are afraid of, you are actually manifesting more fear.

And so, return your focus to love, to the thought, How may I serve? Know that when you serve and when you love, your path will open up before you. For although you may have chosen to experience challenges in your life, for every density you have experienced, there is the opposite end of the spectrum. There is light, hope, contentment and satisfaction that you are meant to enjoy as well. Love brings you into alignment with these victories. Choose love and move forward. Open your heart and share compassion. And this will bring you into alignment with who you really are and why you are really here. Know that, yes, you are needed. You are necessary. Your purpose makes a difference.

Honor your dreams, honor your inspirations, and take action to bring them into being. You may not see it, but accomplishing even a small victory brings you to a place where you more effortlessly manifest your next step, your next goal, or your next intention. If you are guided to do something and you do not understand why, if it feels good and exciting and you can bring it about through the path of love and compassion, then create. Take action!

From this new point you have reached, another window will open up. You will not see the whole path at once, but trust and move forward. Like following a bouncing ball of light, your path will appear before you one step at a time. As you take that step, the next will open up. And as you take that one, more will be known to you.

I, Archangel Gabriel, am always near. And I am happy to

assist you in cultivating your inner creativity, so you may use this to create blessings in your life and for the physical realm in general. Blessings come from your love and your compassion. Be willing to serve. Be willing to love and the rest will open up for you one step at a time. Take that next step, and then you will be further inspired to move in the direction of your ultimate goal.

You have been cleansed and lifted. Now open your heart and allow your creativity to shine through. You are so dearly loved and blessed, and we leave you now with our blessing. Goodbye for now.

5

Healing through Forgiveness

~Archangel Metatron

"Forgive and, with this giving of your forgiveness, you are able to heal. Your vibration actually increases, healing happens for you on a cellular level and an energetic level."

~ Archangel Metatron

Beloved one, indeed I, Archangel Metatron, greet you along with your unique team of guides and angels, with the energy of love, compassion, kindness, and forgiveness. Our focus now is lifting you up and assisting you in tuning into the powerful force of healing made available through forgiveness.

First, we focus your conscious awareness on you, spiritual being in physical form. Draw your attention to anywhere you seek forgiveness from yourself. Where have you fallen short in your opinion? Where have you failed to reach a goal of your heart? What have you done? Where have you failed to try?

Let the awareness of where you need forgiveness come to your attention now. It can be something real or something perceived. Perhaps you desire to forgive yourself for a way you have treated another or even yourself at some phase in your life. Let the time in which you seek forgiveness come to your awareness. Notice the circumstances around this time, and now notice the feeling associated that needs to be released. How did you feel around this time? Let that come to the surface, feel it, and now let it go.

Your angels swoop in around you taking this past feeling and releasing it to the light. And now love, compassion, and forgiveness, indeed, flow your way to fill any void. Let this energy in, let forgiveness in, let self-love in, let compassion in. Let these fill any void in you, filling out your aura and your light body, increasing your vibration; for forgiveness, love and compassion, indeed, hold a high vibration. Ground your light into the Earth, anchoring the power of forgiveness into the planet to benefit you and the collective field of all that is.

Breathe and affirm aloud or in your mind, I love and approve myself. I forgive myself. All is well. I am safe. The power of these words nourishes your energetic and physical body. The self-love you are able to vocally express now nurtures the cellular structure of your body. And so let this healing light in. Now feel your awareness ground down through the bottom of your feet, grounding this self-love, forgiveness, and light into physical form.

And now we encourage you to allow your awareness to focus on someone outside of you who has hurt you. Where is forgiveness for others needed in order for you to complete your healing journey? Now allow your awareness to turn to where another has brought you pain or discomfort or challenge, where you have felt manipulated or brushed aside. Let this come into your awareness now. This person, place, or circumstance may have hurt you in the recent past or distant past.

Let it come up for you now, and energetically speaking, we angels invite the higher spirit of the persons where forgiveness is needed to come in. And now imagine that you and they are in a round circular room with light all around. This is a sacred space that transcends place and time. And so you are able to invoke and invite anyone whom you may forgive or be forgiven by. Understand that forgiveness is for them, yes, so they may release and continue on their healing journey. But so too is it for you so you may release the cord and pain and hurt of the past.

Forgive and, with this giving of your forgiveness, you are able to heal. Your vibration actually increases, healing happens for you on a cellular level and an energetic level. As you let go of any grievance held against you, think or say now, I forgive you. Think of this person in need of forgiveness and offer it to them now. We angels move in to wrap in our wings of love the pain or discomfort or hurt or challenge in this situation, to lift it up and out of you and out of this person you are remembering, releasing all the pain and hardship and dense energy into the light.

And now, in the sacred healing space, an incredible amount of love, compassion, light, and forgiveness flow in. Let this in. Let this fill you. Gracefully share it with the other who is on your mind, who is in most need. Let this forgiveness cycle occur. The forgiveness energy serves them and it serves you; for pain and fear are released so that love, compassion, and forgiveness will take their place.

The vibration of every cell in your body is able to automatically increase with this simple shift of perspective, with forgiveness. Shift away from holding onto past wounds to forgiving and returning to love with this simple action. Lift in vibration and ground this new level of love, compassion, light, and understanding into the Earth, which is connected to everyone and everything, to all that is. The forgiveness you allow to enter into you and into the Earth now brings profound healing on a subtle level. It is on the subtle level energetically that great shifts are able to be initiated.

And so now, dearest one, we draw your attention to humanity as a whole, to the greater collective conscious, to all that is. Let this group consciousness, this mass consciousness come into your awareness. Where is forgiveness needed? Where have you judged and failed to love the greater whole of humanity? Where have you been hurt or scarred or betrayed by humans? Divine beings are at the core but are under a veil of illusion where mind and ego and judgment are still prevalent. And so where have you been hurt by this greater whole of humanity, of the collective consciousness? Feel, remember, sense, know this past pain or hurt that in a way has still been stored within you on a cellular level, limiting the full vibration you are able to lift. Hand it over to the angels present here now and release into the light.

And so, right now, by being aware of past hurts that you are still holding onto, you can scan your physical body. Where is the remaining dense energy? Where is the stuck energy? Where is the pain? Zoom into this area and ask, what is this pain tied to? Is it past hurt? Where is forgiveness needed? Whatever vibration, emotion, or feeling is tied to your past hurt and comes up now, dive into it. Let yourself feel it fully, let yourself remember what it felt like to be judged, to be betrayed, to be hurt.

Now release this over to your angels, who wrap you in wings of love and take all this past pain, hurt, suffering, and doubt and release it into the light. Now forgiveness, love, and compassion flow your way. Let them in. Let them fill this void, repairing your cells, repairing your aura, lifting you in vibration. Indeed, now ground all this light, forgiveness, love and compassion into the core of the Earth, claiming it for yourself and for the greater collective consciousness of all that is.

You see, forgiveness brings great benefit into your life and into the lives of others. When you forgive, this healing energy becomes a part of your vibrational energy signature, which does not end with you but intermixes with all that is. Through even subtle, slight advancements on your part with clearing of past hurts and wounds, and forgiving those who have betrayed or caused harm in your life, you are able to create a significant shift. Gladly release pain and readily absorb the love and compassion, which is broadcast your way in return. And when you ground this into the Earth, it becomes available and accessible by all. Forgiveness is one of the most powerful healing vibrations available.

And so once more, now in a more general sense, quiet your mind, open your heart, and tune in to your physical, emotion, mental, and spiritual being. Where are you are still holding onto past hurt and to feelings of being unloved, of judgment, or not being accepted? Tune into this, do not be afraid, do not suppress, and do not bury it. Simply tune in, notice the feeling. Did you even know it was still stored in you?

Dive in, let yourself feel it now. Let yourself feel what you felt like then, knowing now you can release it. Let the past wound appear and then let it go; release it over to the angels and into the light. As if holding something in your hand and just dropping it, let it go now. Invite forgiveness to take its place, forgiveness for you, and for all who have caused you hurt and harm. Love and compassion also flow your way. Now ground these vibrations in to the Earth. And so, it is.

You may wish to repeat an affirmation to help continue facilitating the healing and forgiveness process. This affirmation can be used to bring healing energy into a room. Or you may place your hands over a specific part of your body or on the back of a loved one, as you simply say or think: I love you. I'm sorry for anything I may have done consciously or unconsciously to cause you harm. Please forgive me. Thank you. I love you. When you offer forgiveness to others as needed, you complete the healing loop.

But for now, just focus on you. Affirm: I love you. I'm sorry for anything I may have done consciously or unconsciously to cause you harm. Please forgive me. Thank you. I love you. Feel your energy open up, as you say or even read these words. Feel your energy open up as forgiveness, the most powerful healing force available to you besides love, flows into your awareness. Let forgiveness nurture your being. Unite with forgiveness for self and for others.

You may wish to tune in once more now. Who else do you need to forgive? Where else is a grudge or past density or a simple memory of a hurtful time holding you back from moving forward and stepping into your full light? Tune in to this now, to a person, a situation. And what is the essential element that caused you pain or hurt or suffering? Let yourself feel this now. Remember what it felt like to be in that position.

And now release the dense, heavy, painful emotion, memory; let it go. Release it into the light and let compassion, forgiveness, and love take hold, take its place, illuminating you, repairing your energetic field, lifting you in vibration for love, compassion, and forgiveness. Indeed, illuminate. Now ground this light into your physical life, and ground love, compassion and forgiveness into your reality. So you may benefit from these vibrations, and all of humanity, all of the collective consciousness, and all that is may forgive, may love, and may move forward on the path of joy and vibrant living.

Dearest, I am Archangel Metatron. I leave you with my blessing and with an immense amount of love, compassion, and forgiveness, which is always available to you. Use it often and use it as needed. Love others, have compassion for others, graciously forgive others, and you will continue to lift and open and rise. Remember to ground your light in to Earth and know that all is well.

I, Metatron, leave you now with my blessing, with love, with compassion, and with forgiveness. Goodbye for now.

6

Release
and Rebirth

~ Archangel Michael

"Love is the root to accomplishing your goal of being here in the physical, of integrating your full power from many lives, from many tales, from many times."

~ Archangel Michael

Greetings, beloved one. I, Archangel Michael, greet you in this moment and say to you "All is well." And so for now, relax. Relax your face, your neck, and your shoulders, arms, hands. Relax your legs and your feet. Relax your toes and your fingers. And now feel your energy ground, flowing down, connecting with Earth, and thereby connecting with all that is. Relax.

Now imagine a bright light shining down on you from above—light from the Divine and light from angelic beings of light beyond the veil, who are right now broadcasting light streams to planet Earth. Some of these flow to places on your planet where there is density, where there has been war, where there is great suffering, and towards those who are experiencing hardship or poverty. Some of these streams flow to those who are experiencing a broken heart, to heal the wounds of the heart and return to love. Some of these streams carry new souls from the realm of spirit into the physical vibration. And some of these streams of light assist those in your realm who are ready to return to the full light of spirit beyond the physical, who are ready to die in the physical sense, leaving behind the physical body and life, returning fully into the light.

You see, we angels are always working behind the scenes to assist humanity in lifting. We are here to assist planet Earth in experiencing a rebirth, shifting into a paradigm of love, gratitude and compassion. We see these things as being possible, as the primary mode of relating to one another on your planet. But, for this to come about, the old must die and fade away. Know that all is divinely timed, and all is in divine order.

Even the density you see happening in the world around you, the sorrow broadcast for all to view, is coming up now so you, as one light, one consciousness, one humanity, can turn away from reveling in the suffering of others. You can learn to respond with love and compassion and can, ultimately, heal yourself as a collective whole, healing consciousness as one unit.

You see, each individual does make a difference. Each individual plays an essential part in making up the greater whole. And so, as one individual heals beliefs of hate, patterns of destruction, and shifts the overall lens of viewing reality from a negative perspective, all are impacted.

As one person, you become consciously aware of your surroundings and your true light, and all are affected. As you evolve and shift, as you let fade away that which no longer serves, and you step boldly into your new life, you are reborn as a spiritual master of love and compassion, and all are affected by this. With your awareness, the scales are tipped, and consciousness is encouraged on the collective and the personal level. Others make the shift, release negativity, heal, and to return to love.

Feel the light of the Divine above you now, flowing or pouring upon you. Breathe and relax to consciously open, to let light in from above, and to let light lift you. From below, the light at the core of the Earth flows up towards you. Golden light from the Divine, light from above and light from below pour into you. Allow this light to enter and to flow throughout your being.

Let yourself be aware of any physical symptoms of pain or density that you have been experiencing recently. Like a magnet, light will automatically flow to those exact areas. You must be willing to let go of pain, but with your permission, a powerful release can occur now. Let go. Let pain and tension dissolve into the light, which is called in all around you, through simply reading these words.

Now, let your awareness be drawn into the areas where you still feel tension or pain stored, and open your heart. Know, feel or understand what caused this pain. What is the root? What is the thought process or the lesson connected to how you are feeling?

For pain does have its purpose. Pain seeks to bring to consciousness that which is unknown. Those beliefs in you that do not serve will manifest in your body as pain to be finally acknowledged. When you release the impressions of negativity that you have taken upon your being, pain is released. This is easy to do.

In every interaction you have with another, your energy signature shifts in a good way when you are laughing, you are in joy, or you have a love-filled relationship. However, if you are scolded, reprimanded, or if you engage in an argument and get angry, fearful or sad, this too affects your vibration and more. It affects the energy signature that you broadcast in every moment, the energy you contribute to the whole of collective consciousness.

This is why so many masters before you have said, "respond with love," "choose love in the moment," "love is the way, the truth and the light," "love is your path to full awakening." These things have been said because they are true. When another approaches you with negativity, and you respond with love, your love shields you, your aura, your physical body, and your light. You are shielded by love so you can then contribute compassion, gratitude, hope and healing to the other.

You do not need to absorb hooks or attachments or imprints of negativity from the world around you. If you have absorbed some of these energies thus far, the process is simple. First, tune into the pain. Tune into the tension stored in your physical body and let the strands of light, the light waves broadcast from light beings in the angelic realm, flow to these locations.

Let the light from the Divine enter in and flow throughout your body, mind, and spirit. Relax to allow light to enter into the places where you have absorbed the energies of another. Let the light enter into the places where your own negativity and thought has caused a blockage. Let light cycle and flow throughout you, bringing up, washing up, pulling out, dissolving and releasing into the light all negative vibrations and emanations that are not yours. Let them go. Let them flow effortlessly out of storage in your cellular memory, in your energetic body, or in your physical being, and let them release into the light.

Now imagine that the orb of light is once again above you. Let yourself feel illuminated as millions of droplets of light now begin to flow down. Millions of strands of light entering into the physical, all focused on you. All focused on you in this very moment to take away, release, or dissolve whatever has come up for you into the light.

Whatever pain you have taken hold of in your life has been embraced and allowed in. For although it may have come as a result of an interaction with another, you are ultimately one, responsible for your own energy and how you react. It is the others' energy combined with your reaction that causes, in the case of negative attachment, hooks or cords to take hold and nest and grow in you. Left unattended, these negative imprints can turn into a sort of possession, and they can seriously weigh you down.

In this now moment, be willing to let whatever you need to know, regarding energies you have taken on from others, come into your awareness. What is your lesson in all of this? Is it practicing boundaries and knowing when to say no? Or is it simply releasing your own past hurts and, in every moment, consciously returning to love and compassion? The lesson is, let density go. Let light take its place, and enter in. Open your heart wide. Focus inward on your inner still, calm peace.

From this inner perspective, imagine now that you are being transported to a beautiful place in nature, your inner sanctuary of the natural world. As you arrive in this beautiful location, you notice the sun is just beginning to set. With your consciousness, you choose to bring in the element of fire by lighting a candle or building a small fire before you.

As the sun continues to set, notice the colors that illuminate the surroundings—peaches, golden hues, purple light. Notice that it is winter where you are, as Earth too pulls back her energy in decline, in letting go of past wounds and suffering; pulling back the energy, focusing it inward, reflecting, honoring the journey, preparing for spring, and preparing for growth. A part of healing through rebirth is pausing and reflecting, honoring what has been and what will come.

Focus your awareness on the flame or fire burning before you. With your mind's eye, view the light of the flames flickering, warming you, and in a way, healing a part of you. As the Earth around you becomes darker, moving towards night, the fire remains bright and comforting, bringing you hope. The fire reminds you of the flame, of the light, which burns brightly within your own heart.

Notice that you are still aware of the visualization of flames dancing about before you. Now focus inward once more on your heart and on the fire, the flame or inner light, which burns therein. This flame of love, the flame of the Divine is your true nature. Your true nature is divine love. Let this burn within you. Let this glow. Let this divine flame, this divine love within you expand and illuminate your entire being with light.

The new beginning you are approaching happens, in a way, on the collective scale but is only made possible through your life and your experience. And so, open and lift in these flames of love that dance within you, which will carry you forward into your new beginning. It is important for you to keep your awareness on that which you desire, on the future you are willing to create.

Do not remain focused on your fears or worries about your goals not working out. There is a saying of being the devil's advocate, of looking at the negatives, of exploring the contrast and the duality of situations. I, Archangel Michael, say to you, this does not serve.

It is OK to recognize doubt that creeps up. Pause for a moment, tune into the doubt and ask yourself, Is this truly from what I am seeking to manifest, or is this simply residue arising from past fears or uncertainties?

What answers do you receive? What do you feel? Is it from the present or is it from the past? If it is past, let it go. If it is a real fear, ask, does this feeling mean that what I am trying to manifest is not in line with my true authentic desires? Or is it simply fear? Am I hearing my ego mind? Is it the part of me that wants to remain small, still scared and alone? Let yourself know that, with awareness, you are able to release all doubt and fear. Ask yourself, am I willing to let it go? Could I let it go? When will I let it go?

We advise now: Release and let doubt exit your being, releasing into the light, flowing up on the strands of love broadcast from the angels who gladly accept it. Angels will transform this energy back into love and back into a pattern of flow that can serve humanity and serve all. Love is the path into the new paradigm. Love is the key to accomplishing your goal for being here in the physical, of integrating your full power from many lives, from many tales, from many times.

Now is the time for you to bring the whole wisdom and history of your soul into this present moment, to love, to anchor light into the physical for the benefit of Earth and all creatures and all beings. Now is the time for you to play your part in assisting humanity in turning away from the message of fear and negativity broadcast by your media in your world, and claiming the new Earth for yourself, claiming a new life for yourself, and living with the certainty of joy, trust, hope and understanding.

Your true nature is divine love. Ponder this as, once again, your awareness through these words is drawn to the visualization of a fire burning before you. The fire is illuminating the darkness of the night. The fire is reminding you that this same light, this same divine essence brightly burns within you. But what kindles your fire is not wind and wood. What kindles your fire is love and a willingness to enter in, to open your heart, to fan the flame of love with your breath, through breathing in love, light and compassion. And as you exhale, let the light of the Divine and the love of your heart and soul flow out, impressing upon your energy signature, unconditional love.

Love will heal any negative imprints you may have received.

Continue flowing out pure love and compassion and hope to the collective consciousness and energy field. Love is a valid contribution, and so, yes, we encourage you to choose love in every moment.

When you find you are being challenged, and love is the last resort, the last thing you could see yourself responding with, step back. Enter in and breathe to kindle the flame of your heart and take the road less traveled. The easy route is not the master path to success. It is easy to judge, to doubt and to fear. But the road less traveled, the master path is responding with love and compassion, despite whatever is going on around you. To respond to your outer world with presence and with love is the greatest gift. Through love you claim the full power of this point of new beginning.

There are so many beings of light, angels, ascended masters, guides, and fairies, who are currently broadcasting love, hope, and compassion towards the physical realm. These beings seek to assist humanity in turning the corner and allowing harsh density and judgment to die and fade away. Let this light from the Divine into your experience to claim your power to rebirth yourself into the new paradigm. Enter into an entirely new experience of a higher level.

Time will show the full change on planet Earth, but right now, through your perspective, you can see that all is new. Allow yourself to turn away from the doubts, from worries and focus on what you desire to see manifest. Your thoughts are supercharged now. Your manifestation abilities are increased.

This is not to say that you can only dream, hope, and intend what you desire to see, and it will be; for your action is still required. By aligning intention with being in the right place at the right time or meeting the right people to help you accomplish your goals, the puzzle pieces will certainly fall into place with increasing speed. As you first plant seeds of thought and clear intention, you then take action as inspired to bring your vision into being.

All is well. Honor yourself as your past struggles begin to arise and fade away. They come up for review and to be released. Look at the struggle, do not hide from it. Remember the tragedy, the pain you have experienced, for we are not saying it is not real. Understand the challenges and feelings you have suffered through in this life, and then let them go. Be willing to release pain into the light and return your focus to love. This brings your point of attraction into alignment with the truth of who you are, divine spirit burning brightly with divine love.

Now returning to the visualization where you are in your sacred space in nature, look up. Notice all of the stars brightly shining down. One star in particular catches your eye, as it is brighter than the rest. Imagine that from this star, your team of guides and angels, who have been with you from your birth and will be with you throughout this life, are broadcasting whatever you most need. Light frequency, healing, hope, understanding are beaming down upon you. You may feel like you are lifting, as this light channels through you and pours down upon you.

Embrace what your guides send, open your heart, the rose of divine love within you. And now feel all of this light you have connected with ground. Ground your awareness into the Earth. Feel your energy flowing down into the core of Earth where you can feel, know and experience that you are not separate. Experience and feel that you are one with the Earth and all that is.

You are one with the light from the Divine that flows in from above, and the light from the core of the Earth flows in from below. Let these two lights meet at your heart, rekindling this flame so it brightly burns within you. With this light, sharing love and compassion with those around you comes easily and naturally.

Take in another breath of air, and let it flow throughout your being. Let healing, light and love effortlessly flow throughout your body. When you breathe out, let all this light flow out to the Earth, to consciousness, to all.

Repeat this visualization and know that I, Archangel Michael, am always near. You are so dearly loved and supported, as you let fade away that which no longer serves, and as you rebirth yourself into a new being with new eyes of love.

You are able to make a difference in each moment. Choose love, choose hope, and begin to plant the seeds of intention about what you desire to see manifest in the new beginning, in the new Earth. Set your intentions, ask for help and take action as inspired. Be willing to let go of the old to let new blessings in, for now is the time to rebirth yourself into experiencing the full divine love that you are. You are love, and you are so loved.

We need you now to shine your light to complete the loop, to broadcast your energy signal, which will interact with the collective whole. One moment at a time, your world is shifting away from fear and into love. You are an important component in this transition. Be willing, for love serves all.

I, Archangel Michael, leave you with my blessing and with love. Let it in. Goodbye for now.

7

Return Home to Consciousness and to Love

~ Archangel Metatron

"It is essential for the awakening and transformation of all humanity on your planet that you shine your unique light."

~ Archangel Metatron

Indeed, beloved, we are here. And I, Metatron, am so pleased to connect with you now. You are, of course, surrounded with the energy of the light, and yet, you also have bright light shining within you in the form of your inner fire, your open heart.

And so, now tune in to this inner light and power radiantly and brightly shining within you. Draw your breath in and feel your in-breath gently fanning the flame of fire within your heart chakra. Allow the light of your heart to grow and build, and as you exhale now, let this light, this blessing of well-being and love and peace, radiate throughout your body, throughout the room you are in, throughout your Earth, and all that is.

Breathe in and allow your inner light to build and grow.

Now breathe out, letting this light flow out from you, blessing all who are near. Imagine light rippling out through consciousness, and know that your awakened energetic signature indeed has the powerful effect of bringing about positive change in your world.

You are, of course, living in a time of great change, and yet you hold within you great power and light to manifest joy and blessings in your life. These blessings are not limited to your own experience, but as you intend positive thoughts when you feel good, this creates a ripple effect. Your light has the ability to extend beyond the present time, beyond this here and now.

From our perspective in the realms of spirit, this powerful work, which you are already engaged in, holds great potential for you to arise awakened and fully empowered to live your divine blueprint, your blessed life now. The light you feel around and within you now is the energy of your angels and guides. You are being enveloped with love, blessed with frequency and spirit. Know that we are not separate from you; we are all one energy, one consciousness.

And now by focusing your awareness within your open heart, your center within, return to this conscious knowing of connection and love throughout all existence. Enter into the realm of love, the space of your heart, and feel the peace, calm and stillness inside. This peace and love always awaits you, it is always a breath away.

In the course of your existence, your mind may find all kinds of scenarios, doubts and fears to bombard you with. But despite whatever is happening in the physical world

Angel Messages: *Breathe and Lift in Angelic Love, Light & Compassion* around you, you always have the choice and the opportunity to breathe and drop into the peace and stillness of your heart. Return home, return to consciousness and love.

And now from this place of inward focus with your breath, notice that you can breathe in any thoughts that are still lingering around you. Your thoughts or thoughts of others spiraling above you are all connected to collective consciousness. Breathe in these thoughts, and return all these thoughts and emotions to the realm of your heart through your in-breath, where they transcend through love.

Through consciousness, you are able to filter all thought through the window of your heart. By returning to consciousness and calming your thoughts, welcome home to the stillness, peace, and divine energy of this now moment. Breathe in thought, and as you breathe out, let your flame of light extend beyond your body. Feel the energy in the room lift, feel your energy lift in vibration as you give of your light to the world, returning all to conscious awareness.

Indeed, your every thought, your emotions and beliefs do not end with you. You are so closely intertwined, from our perspective, with everything in existence. And so, as you ascend, awaken, and claim more of your power to live joyously, free and in love, you succeed by following your passions and flowing your creativity, letting your inner light shine, and letting yourself glow and radiate. You may feel now that your physical body is tingling or shining. You are glowing; you are radiant and vibrant from this place of clear mind and open heart.

With a vibrant physical body and fully awakened spirit, you

are unlimited, limited not. Your mind may think, may present you with limitations, but the truth of your heart and of consciousness is that your every desire, dream or wish for your life and for humanity can come to be. Release all doubt, and let go of the realm of your mind. Let go, breathe and relax. Breathe in all thought, returning the realm of thought and mind home to love, to the void, the place of peace, still and calm.

Relax. There is nowhere you must be, nothing you must do or even think. Simply enjoy this very moment and experience your full connection to your light and your power. And from this place of open heart, vibrant spirit, incredible light, you are able to start a wave, a ripple of conscious thought beginning inward, extending outward, and sharing your blessing, your vision with all.

We see that there is great love and happiness and empowerment awaiting you, to live not following the guidance or ideals of another but following the inner promptings and callings of your heart. Through tuning in and opening your heart, you are able to open this portal within and fully connect with your higher self, with your cosmic light, and your spiritual light body.

And as you do this, bringing more and more of your full energy, your full light, and full awareness into the physical, the benefits will not end with you. Your life can take on the magical synchronicity of being connected to love, and this love will also continue extending outward, offering unlimited blessings of hope and love for Earth and for humanity.

Breathe in again now, noticing the light of divine love still remains all around you. Breathe in this light to further activate and awaken your core, your spirit. Notice a pillar of white light now, flowing through your being, connecting and anchoring all of your chakra energy centers to divine love. It is not ending with your physical body, but extending upward into the universe, into the heavens, and also extending downward, grounding you to earth, to Mother Earth, uniting heavens and earth, divine energy of love filling your heart. Open, enjoy this, and relax into the still and peace and calm of this now.

This inner light, your inner light and peace always awaits. Remember to return to love, to return to consciousness when thoughts of others and the outside world overwhelm. Breathe them in, return thought to conscious love, return to the still, calm knowing of your divinity, of your power, of your full spiritual nature and energy. You are physical, but you are also spiritual. And with your clear mind and open heart, you are able to access all of your creative potential now.

This light, again, does not stop with you. It continues through all of existence. You each have a great potential and ability to bring about positive change in the world. Focus not on the challenges you and humanity face, but rather focus on your light, your love and let your creative voice, your divine energy signature play out in the world around you.

It is essential for the awakening and transformation of all humanity on your planet that you shine your unique light. You are here now because you are a way-shower and you have the ability to help others. For all to awaken on earth, your story is needed, is essential for all to reach the tipping point where love and consciousness are known, are experienced, and are balanced in love and peace.

Feel your energy lift once more, as we flow even more cosmic love into your energy field. Accept this, if you would like, according to your highest and greatest good. You may feel this light flowing or tingling, or just be relaxed and calm. Whatever you feel is OK. Let it be OK, and know that you are receiving a divine blessing and initiation.

Nothing holds you back from sharing this light with the world. Follow the inner nudge and prompting of your heart to create, to express, to share your story. This is all you must do. Follow your heart's guidance, and from your open heart, you will even increase your divine connection to your full spirit and light and power.

The magic, the love, the divine blessing that you can open to and experience here in physical form, connected to your spirit, is unlimited. Be joyous, celebrate, have fun and play, and know you are so loved and supported and encouraged to let your full light shine. You are already shining brightly, but where do you hold back? Where do you follow another, instead of following your own knowing and truth and path?

You are the way, you are the truth, you are the light, and you are connected to all that is. As you realize this and trust in this truth and connection, and allow yourself to create positive change in the greater field of awareness and consciousness, the fulfillment and love and blessing you seek will be known.

Notice your physical body once again now and draw more light into your physical self with your breath. As you exhale, let go of any tension, any negativity, or any fear, which is stored in your body physically or even at the cellular level. Let go. Breathe in again, replacing the void where you have released, with light and with love.

Now go forth shining your light in your unique way, letting your full spiritual self play in physical existence. You are blessed to be here now, creator on earth. Let your creativity flow, let your divine light awaken and be fully illuminated. You are divine. Claim this light.

You matter; your work of returning to consciousness, returning to love, returning to the present moment extends far beyond your life. You are ushering in the new paradigm on Earth, the emerging new humanity centered in love and joy. Claim this first in your own life and experience the ripple effect, which extends infinitely outward.

We leave you now with our blessing, with energy, and with the reminder that within you all things are possible by staying connected to your inner light and conscious awareness. All knowledge, all wisdom, all healing you need is there. Simply open and allow this light, this cosmic energy to flow in and through you to serve. Stay in joy, beloved, for your happiness serves you and serves all. Your love has infinite power to create blessings, positive change and hope in your life and the lives of others.

You are cleansed, you are blessed, and you are infinitely loved. Accept now a token from your angels—a gift. Let this come in to your awareness now, the present from these divine beings who are always near.

What your angels offer you now may seem subtle or small. Accept it energetically into your aura, if it feels good to you, and go forth in love: I am willing to receive blessings from the Divine

And we leave you now with infinite blessings. Goodbye for now.

Additional Resources

Your 2 Free .MP3 Angel Meditations

1. Connecting With Your Angels, Guides & Higher Self ~ .MP3 Angel Message with Archangel Metatron

2. Manifesting With Love ~ .MP3 Angel Message with Archangel Uriel

Visit http://www.ask-angels.com/love/ to download your bonus angel messages.

Connect with Us on YouTube!
http://www.youtube.com/askangels

Join Us on Facebook!
https://www.facebook.com/AskAngelsFan

Let Your Light Shine

Open your heart and mind to experience the unconditional love and guidance of the Angelic Realm. Simply reading these messages from the angels will assist you in bringing more joy, healing, and spiritual fulfillment into your life. With the guidance and uplifting angelic frequency woven throughout these pages, you will be inspired to Let Your Light Shine!

http://www.amazon.com/dp/B00AA59U9W

Experience Angels

Experiencing angels is simple once you know how to make the connection. Simply relax and read as Archangel Uriel, Archangel Metatron, Archangel Michael and the Angelic Guide Orion walk you through the process of activating and opening your chakras, lifting your vibration, and connecting with your Guardian Angels. Then rise even higher to experience your Higher Self and the realm of the Archangels. This book will help you pave the pathway so that you can directly connect with the Angelic Realms, to Experience Angels for yourself.

http://www.amazon.com/dp/B00G8UVIAM

Ascension Angel Messages

Ascension is the path of love and is available for all who are willing to consciously evolve through aligning with higher consciousness and with the Divine. As you read the channeled angel messages by Melanie in this book, you will experience angelic healing, love and light, which will assist you in progressing on your ascension path.

http://www.amazon.com/dp/1500968862

Basics of Numerology

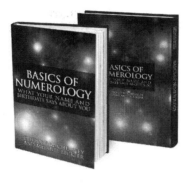

Delve into the fascinating world of numerology to learn what your name and birth date say about you. In this co-authored book by Melanie and Clifford Cheasley, you will learn to calculate your personal numbers for which the vibrational meaning provides insight into your personality, soul urge, appearance, as well as your life path.

http://www.amazon.com/dp/B00LH2Z2EY

Made in the USA
Monee, IL
03 May 2024